The First Book of Mezzo-Soprano/Alto Solos

COMPLETE
Parts I, II, and III

ISBN 978-1-4803-3322-2

Complete Package released 2013

G. SCHIRMER, Inc.

DISTRIBUTED BY

HAL•LEONARD®
CORPORATION
7777 W. BLUEMOUND RD. P.O. BOX 13819 MILWAUKEE, WI 53213

www.musicsalesclassical.com
www.halleonard.com

THE
FIRST
BOOK OF
MEZZO-SOPRANO/ALTO
SOLOS
PART I

PREFACE

Repertoire for the beginning voice student, whether teenager, college student, or adult, always poses a great challenge for the voice teacher because of the varied abilities and backgrounds the students bring to the studio. This series of books for soprano, mezzo-soprano and alto, tenor, and baritone and bass provides a comprehensive collection of songs suitable for first and second year students of any age, but is compiled with the needs of the young singer in mind.

In general, students' first experiences with songs are crucial to their further development and continued interest. Young people like to sing melodious songs with texts they can easily understand and with accompaniments that support the melodic line. As the student gains more confidence, the melodies, the texts, and the accompaniments can be more challenging. I have found that beginning students have more success with songs that are short. This enables them to overcome the problems of musical accuracy, diction, tone quality, proper technique, and interpretation without being overwhelmed by the length of the song.

Each book in this series includes English and American songs, spirituals, sacred songs, and an introduction to songs in Italian, German, French and Spanish. Many students study Spanish in the schools today, and most studio volumes do not include songs in this language; therefore, we have included two for each voice type.

Several songs in the collections have been out of print in recent years, while others have been previously available only in sheet form. Special care has been taken to avoid duplication of a great deal of general material that appears in other frequently used collections. These new volumes, with over thirty songs in each book, are intended to be another viable choice of vocal repertoire at a very affordable price for the teacher and student.

Each book contains several very easy beginning songs, with the majority of the material rated easy to moderately difficult. A few songs are quite challenging musically, but not strenuous vocally, to appeal to the student who progresses very rapidly and who comes to the studio with a great deal of musical background.

In general, the songs are short to medium in length. The ranges are very moderate, yet will extend occasionally to the top and the bottom of the typical voice. The majority of the accompaniments are not difficult, and are in keys that should not pose major problems. The variety of texts represented offers many choices for different levels of individual student interest and maturity.

In closing, I wish to thank Richard Walters at Hal Leonard Publishing for allowing me to be part of this effort to create this new series of vocal collections. We hope that these books will fill a need for teachers and students with suitable, attractive and exciting music.

Joan Frey Boytim

CONTENTS

AMERICAN LULLABY

words and music by
Gladys Rich

Hush-a - bye, you sweet lit-tle ba - by, And don't you cry__ an-y

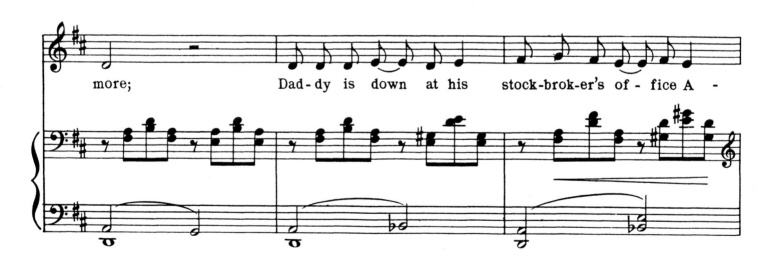

more; Dad-dy is down at his stock-brok-er's of - fice A -

keep-ing the wolf___ from the door.

Nurs-ie will raise the win-dow shade high, So you can see___ the

cars whiz-zing by.___ Home in a hur - ry each Dad-dy must fly___ To a

ba - by like you.

Hush - a - bye, you sweet lit - tle ba - by, And

close those pret - ty blue eyes. Moth-er has gone to her

week-ly bridge par - ty To get her wee ba - by the prize.

8

L'ANNEAU D'ARGENT
(The Silver Ring)

Cécile Chaminade

10

DIE BEKEHRTE
(The Converted One)

Johann Wolfgang von Goethe

Max Stange

Andantino.

Bei dem Glanz der A - bend - rö - the ging ich still den
As I roam'd the woods at lei - sure In the eve - ning

Wald ent - lang,
hour so still,

Da - mon sass und
Da - mon sat and

blies die Flö - te, dass es von den Fel - sen klang:
piped for plea - sure, E - cho an - swer'd from the hill:

so la re
so la re

DER BLUMENSTRAUSS
(The Nosegay)

Felix Mendelssohn

20

THE CHERRY TREE

Margaret Rose

Armstrong Gibbs

Time of performance 2–2¼ mins.

The sad, sweet birds of the Spring -
time are sing - ing a - gain to me.
They sing of the fro - zen riv - ers,

Pi - ping soft and low _____ Till I

think I hear_____ your foot - steps danc - ing

poco rit. *3* a tempo

a - cross the snow.

poco rit.   *mp* a tempo

24

Sing of my love in the North-land _____ As my love once

sang to me. _____

Hush, birds! the cher-ry in si - lence Is

CHI VUOL LA ZINGARELLA

Giovanni Paisiello

so bene in-do-vi - nar.
Their fortune I can tell;

I giovani al can - to - ne
The laddies at the inn,— too,

so meglio stuzzi - car. A vecchi in-na-mo-ra-ti scal - dar fo le cer-
I can amuse as well. When old men feel love burning, I set their heads a -

vel -la, scal - dar fo le cer - vel -la, a vecchi inna-mo-ra-ti. Chi
turning, I set their heads a - turn-ing, When old men feel love burn - ing. Who'll

vuol la zin-ga - rel -la, chi vuol la zin-ga - rel-la? Si - gnori, ec - co-la
try the Gip-sy pretty, Who'll try the Gip-sy pretty? Come one and all to

CLOUD-SHADOWS

Katharine Pyle

James H. Rogers

Slowly and dreamily

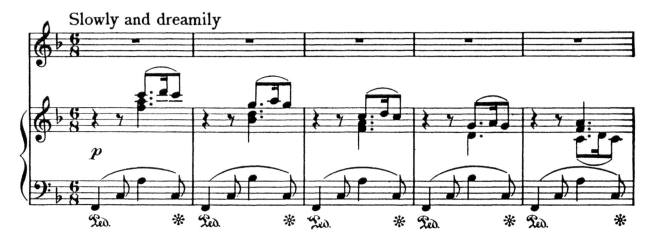

I wish I could ride on the shad-ows of clouds That drift a-cross the

hill; O-ver the mead-ow and out of sight They sweep so smooth and still.

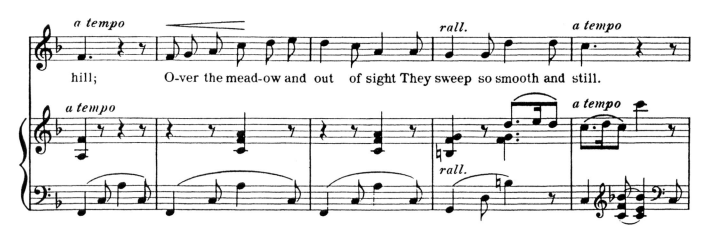

O - ver the dai - sy field they passed, And not a dai - sy stirr'd; They

moved like char - i - ots grand and slow, But nev - er a sound was heard.

wish I could ride on the shad-ows of clouds, Could ride till, the jour - ney done, I'd

find my-self at the end of the world, Where the earth and the sky are one.

CHRISTOPHER ROBIN IS SAYING HIS PRAYERS
(Vespers)

A. A. Milne

H. Fraser-Simson

36

CRABBED AGE AND YOUTH

William Shakespeare

Maude Valérie White

CRUCIFIXION

African American spiritual
arranged by John Payne

Grave ♩=56

very simple, with great devotion

They cru-ci-fied my Lord, An' He nev-er said a mum-bal-lin' word. They cru-ci-fied my Lord, An' He nev-er said a mum-bal-lin' word, Not a word, not a word, not a word.

They pierced Him in the side, An' He nev-er said a mum-bal-lin' word.

They pierced Him in the side, An' He nev-er said a mum-bal-lin' word.

Not a word, not a word, not a word. He

bowed His head an' died, An' He nev - er said a mum - bal - lin'

word, He bowed His head an' died, An' He nev - er said a mum - bal - lin'

word, Not a word, not a word, not a word.

EVENSONG

Constance Morgan

Liza Lehmann

46

EL MAJO TIMIDO
(The Timid Majo)

Llega a mi reja y me mira por la noche un majo.
Que en cuanto me ve y suspira se va calle abajo.
¡Ah! Que tío mas tardío,
Si asi se pasa la vida,
Estoy divertida.

At night, under my window, a majo* comes to look at me.
After he sees me, he sighs and goes on his way.
Ah! What a dull man.
If this is how it's going to be,
Some fun I'll have!

* majo is an untranslatable word for a dashing, handsome lover

Enrique Granados

pi - ra se vá ca - lle a - ba - jo

¡Ay que ti - o mas tar - di - o

Sia- si se pa- sa la vi - da es - toy di - ver - ti - da

GO 'WAY FROM MY WINDOW

words and music by
John Jacob Niles

ICI-BAS!
(Here Below)

Sully Prudhomme

Gabriel Fauré

To be sung in parlando style

I - ci - bas les lè - vres ef - fleu - rent Sans
Here be - low, where lips light-ly sev - er And

rien lais-ser de leur ve - lours,
leave no trace of beau - ty's reign,

Je rêve___ aux bai-
I dream_ of kiss - es

sers qui de-meu - rent Tou - jours!_____
fond that for-ev - er Re - main._____

Ped.   ✻

54

I - ci - bas, tous les hom-mes pleu - rent Leurs a - mi-tiés ou leurs a-
Here be-low, men in vain en-deav - or Weep for their love's or friend-ship's

mours, Je rêve aux cou-ples qui de-meu - rent,_____ aux cou-ples qui de-
pain, I dream of lov-ers who for-ev - er,_____ of lov-ers who for-

meu - rent,_____ qui de-meu - rent Tou-
ev - er,_____ who for-ev - er Re-

jours!_____
main._____

THE LAMB

William Blake

Theodore Chanler

JESUS WALKED THIS LONESOME VALLEY

arranged by Gordon Myers

1. Je - sus walked this lone-some val - ley, He had to

walk it by him - self. Oh, no-bod-y else could walk it

for him, He had to walk it by him - self. 2. We must

walk this lone-some val - ley, we have to walk it by our-

selves. Oh,_____ no-bod-y else_____ can walk it

cresc.   *mf*   *decresc.*

for us, we have to walk it by_____ our-

p

selves. 3. We must clasp_____ our hands to-

mp

geth-er, we have to clasp_____ them in the air. Oh,_

cresc.   *mf*

Note: To dramatize 'loneliness', the last two measures
of the accompaniment may be omitted.

THE LASS FROM THE LOW COUNTREE

John Jacob Niles

sor - row! Now she sleeps in the val - ley where the wild - flow - ers nod, And

no one knows she loved him but her - self and God.___ One

morn, when the sun was on the mead, He passed by her door on a

milk-white steed;_ She smil-ed and she spoke, but he paid no heed. Oh,

sor-row, sing sor-row! Now she sleeps in the val-ley where the

wild-flow-ers nod, And no one knows she loved him but her-self and God.__

If you be a lass from the Low Coun-tree, Don't

THE LORD IS MY SHEPHERD

Pyotr Il'yich Tchaikovsky

adapted and arranged by
Richard Maxwell and
Fred Feibel

Psalm 23

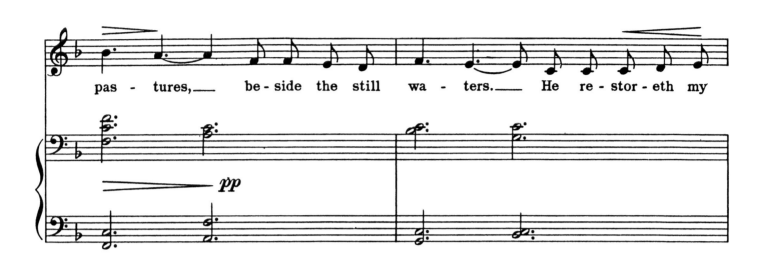

pas - tures,___ be - side the still wa - ters.___ He re - stor - eth my

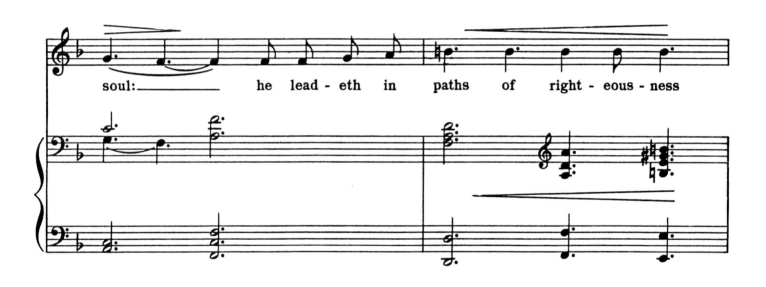

soul:___ he lead - eth in paths of right - eous - ness

for his name's sake.___ Tho' I walk through the val - ley___ of the shad - ow of

68

Sure - ly good - ness and mer - cy shall fol - low me all the

days of my life:_____ and__ I____ will dwell in the house of the

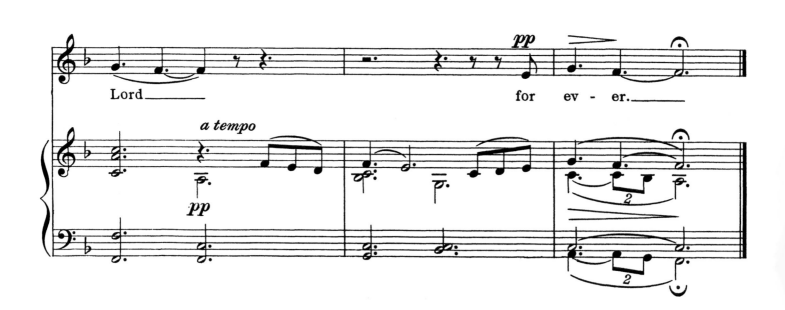

Lord_____ for ev - er._____

SILENT NOON

Dante Gabriel Rossetti

Ralph Vaughan Williams

peace.
The pas-ture gleams and glooms 'Neath bil - low-ing

skies that scat-ter and a - mass.

Poco più mosso

All round our nest, far as the eye can pass, Are

Oh, clasp we to our hearts, for death - less
dower, This close-com-pan - ioned in - ar - tic - u -late hour, When
two - fold si - lence was the song, the
song of love.

LOVELIEST OF TREES

A.E. Housman*

John Duke

*Poem from "A Shropshire Lad." Printed by permission of Grant Richards, London, publisher.

cresc.

poco f

f più animato

Now, of my three - score years and ten.

più animato

mf

Twen - ty will not come a - gain,

MORNING

from the "Atlanta Constitution"
by Frank L. Stanton

Oley Speaks

*From the "Atlanta Constitution;" used by permission.

83

84

PRAYER

Hermann Hagedorn

David W. Guion

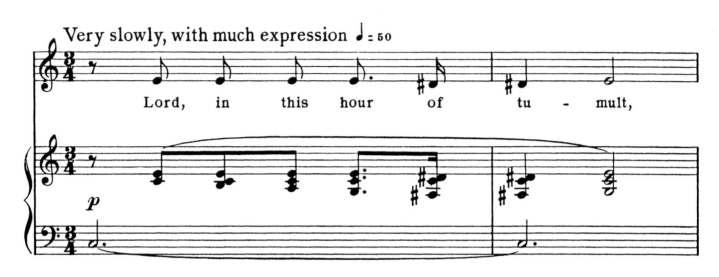

Lord, in this hour of tu - mult,

Lord, in this night of fears,___ Keep o - pen, oh, keep

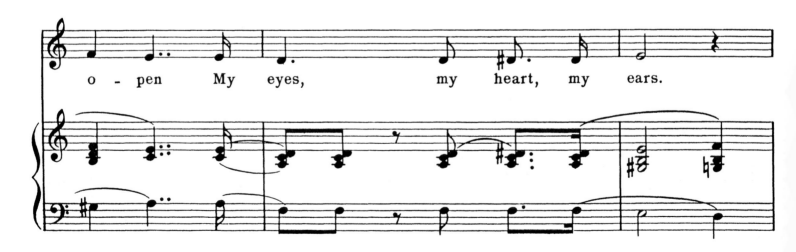

o - pen My eyes, my heart, my ears.

God,   Hear Thou   my plead - ing, Hear Thou   my prayer.

Lord, in   this hour   of   tu - mult,   Lord   in   this night of   fears,___

Keep   o - pen, oh, keep   o - pen   My eyes,   my   ears.

PREGÚNTALE A LAS ESTRELLAS

Latin American folksong
arranged by Edward Kilenyi

Pre -
Go

-gún-ta-le á las flo-res,   si mis a - mo-res les cuen-to   yo,   Cuan-
ask of the sweet flowers bloom-ing   *If of my   sor-rows I   told not   all.*   *Go*

-do la ca-lla-da   no-che cie-rra su bro-che, su-spi - ro   yo,   Pre-
ask of the wild birds   sing-ing   *If I   sigh when the night doth   fall.*   *Go*

-gún-ta-le á las   a-ves,   si tu no sa-bes lo que es a - mor,   Pre-
ask of the dew-y   mea-dows   *If thy love holds not my heart in   thrall.*   *Go*

-gún-ta-le á to-do el pra-do, si no he lu-cha-do con mi do - lor.
ask of all cre - a - tion If for thee, dar-ling, I pine, and call.

colla voce

Tú bien com - pren - des, que yo te quie - ro, Que por tí
Ah! hear me dear - est, how well I love thee, For thee I

mf

colla voce

mue - ro, so - lo por tí; Por-que te quie - ro, bien de mi
per - ish dis-traught with love. My on-ly so - lace is to a-

colla voce

P

cresc.

vi - da, So-lo en el mun-do, so-lo en el mun-do, te quie-ro á ti.____
-dore thee. My heart's de - vo-tion, my heart's de - vo-tion I of-fer thee.____

f

O REST IN THE LORD
from *Elijah*

Psalm 37

Felix Mendelssohn

96

OH SLEEP, WHY DOST THOU LEAVE ME?

from *Semele*

William Congreve

George Frideric Handel

*The Editor's piano accompaniment is founded on Handel's unfigured bass.

OPEN OUR EYES

Frederic West MacDonald

Will C. Macfarlane

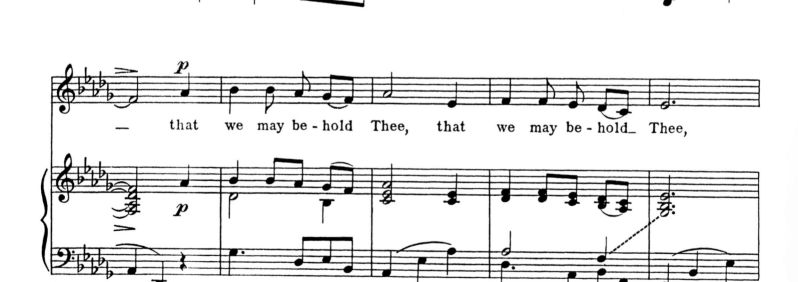

DER SCHWUR
(The Vow)

Erik Meyer-Helmund

Cried Gret-chen to her lov-er: "My dear, you're false to
Es sprach zum Hänschen Gret-chen: "Mein Lie-ben mich ge-

me! With maid-ens fair, all _ o-ver You flirt, so two are we!
reut, du scherzt mit al-len Mäd-chen, wir sind ge-schied'ne Leut'.

Go a-way and leave _ me, No kiss you'll take, Oh, no! Till
Geh deines We-ges wie-der! mein Kuss bleibt dir ver-sagt, bis

THE SKY ABOVE THE ROOF

Mabel Dearmer
based on Verlaine

Ralph Vaughan Williams

The sky a-bove the

roof Is calm and sweet: A tree a-bove the roof Bends

in the heat. A bell from out the blue Drow - si - ly rings: A bird from out the blue Plain - - - tive - ly sings.

110

heart, Poured out in tears? What hast thou

done, O heart,_____ With thy spent years?

colla voce

Più lento.

THE STATUE AT CZARSKOE-SELO

Alexander Pushkin*

Cesar Cui

VOLKSLIEDCHEN
(In The Garden)

Franz Ruckert

Robert Schumann

WIE MELODIEN
(A Thought Like Music)

Klaus Groth

Johannes Brahms

A thought, like mu - sic,__ hold - ing My
Wie Me - lo - di - en__ zieht es mir

heart in soft con - trol, Like flow'rs of spring un-
lei - se durch den Sinn, Wie Früh - lings - blu - men

fold - ing, It thrill - eth through my soul,
blüht es und schwebt wie Duft da - hin,

van - ish quite a - way.
schwin - det wie ein Hauch.

In me - lo - dy ___ deep ___
Und den - noch ruht ___ im ___

hid - den, A fra - grance lies con-cealed, That
Rei - me ver - bor - gen wohl ein Duft, *Den*

bring - eth tears un - bid - den; Un -
mild aus stil - lem Kei - me ein

dim.

TURN THEN THINE EYES

Henry Purcell

catch - ing, catch - ing flames _____ will on __ thy torch ap -

pear, will on thy torch ap - pear, will on thy torch ap -

pear, ap - pear, will on __ thy torch ap - pear will on __ thy torch ap -

Fine

pear pear.

ad lib.

WIND OF THE WESTERN SEA

Alfred Tennyson

Graham Peel

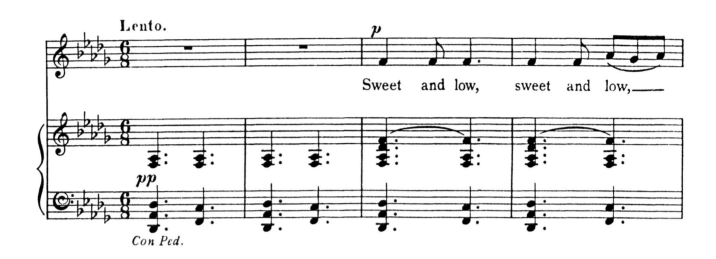

Sweet and low, sweet and low,____

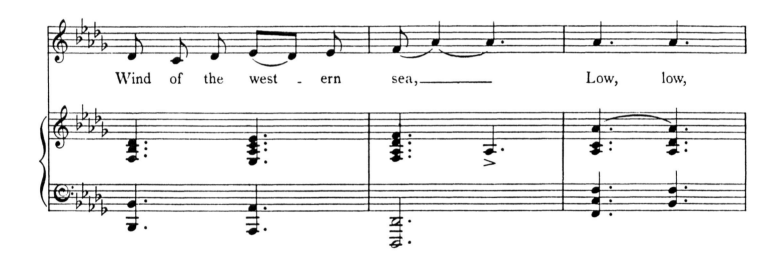

Wind of the west _ ern sea,_____ Low, low,

breathe and blow,____ Wind of the west _ ern sea!_____

O _ ver the roll _ ing wa _ ters go, Come from the dy _ ing

moon, and blow, Blow him a _ gain to me, While my lit _ tle one,

poco rit.

while my pret _ ty one sleeps.___

colla voce   *a tempo*   *p a tempo*   Sleep and rest,

sleep and rest,___ Fa _ ther will come to thee soon;___

Rest, rest on mo_ther's breast,_ Fa_ther will come to thee soon;_

Fa_ther will come to his babe in the nest, Sil _ ver sails_ all

out of the west Un_der the sil_ver moon; Sleep, my lit_tle one,

sleep, my pret _ ty one, sleep._

pp morendo

ppp

THIS LITTLE ROSE

Emily Dickinson*

William Roy

127

THE FIRST BOOK OF MEZZO-SOPRANO/ALTO SOLOS

PART II

PREFACE

The widespread acceptance by teachers and students of "The First Book Series" for Soprano, Mezzo-Soprano/Alto, Tenor, Baritone/Bass has prompted the development of a Part II addition for each voice type. After discussions with numerous voice teachers, the key suggestion expressed many times was that there is a need for "more of the same" type of literature at exactly the same level.

The volumes in Part II follow many of the same concepts which are covered in the Preface of the original volumes, including a comprehensive selection of between 34 and 37 songs from the Baroque through the 20th Century. The selections range from easy to moderate difficulty for both singer and accompanist.

In response to many requests, we have included more sacred songs, and have added two Christmas solos in each volume. The recommendation for more humorous songs for each voice was honored as well.

Even though these books have a heavy concentration of English and American songs, we have also expanded the number of Italian, German, and French offerings. For those using the English singing translations, we have tried to find the translations that are most singable, and in several cases have reworked the texts.

Part II can easily stand alone as a first book for a beginning high school, college, or adult student. Because of the varied contents, Part II can also be successfully used in combination with the first volume of the series for an individual singer. This will give many choices of vocal literature, allowing for individual differences in student personality, maturity, and musical development.

Hal Leonard Publishing (distributor of G. Schirmer) and Richard Walters, supervising editor, have been most generous in allowing the initial objective for this series to be expanded more fully through publishing these companion volumes. We hope this new set of books will provide yet another interesting and exciting new source of repertoire for both the teacher and student.

Joan Frey Boytim
September, 1993

About the Compiler...

Since 1968, Joan Frey Boytim has owned and operated a full-time voice studio in Carlisle, Pennsylvania, where she has specialized in developing a serious and comprehensive curriculum and approach to teaching and coaching adolescent and community adult students. Her teaching experience has also included music and choral instruction at the junior high and senior high levels, and voice instruction at the college level. She is the author of a widely used bibliography, *Solo Vocal Repertoire for Young Singers* (a publication of NATS), and, as a nationally recognized expert on teaching beginning vocal study, has been featured in many speaking engagements and presentations on the subject.

CONTENTS

AH! MIO COR
(Ah! my heart)

English by Theodore Baker

George Frideric Handel

puoi la - sciar - mi, oh De - i, per - chè? per-
canst thou leave me, O Heav-en, and why? and

chè? per - chè? puoi la - sciar - mi so - la in pian - to, oh
why? and why? canst thou leave me weeping, lone - ly, O

De - i! puoi la - sciar - mi, oh De - i, per - chè?
Heav - en! canst thou leave me, O Heav - en, and why?

AS I WENT A-ROAMING

Helen Taylor

May H. Brahe

Printed in the USA by G. Schirmer, Inc.

He said, "You shall walk in a gown made of satin, A ring on your finger, a rose at your ear; And you shall ride forth in a coach with six horses, And I'll love you truly, if you'll be my dear. Derry derry down derry oh!

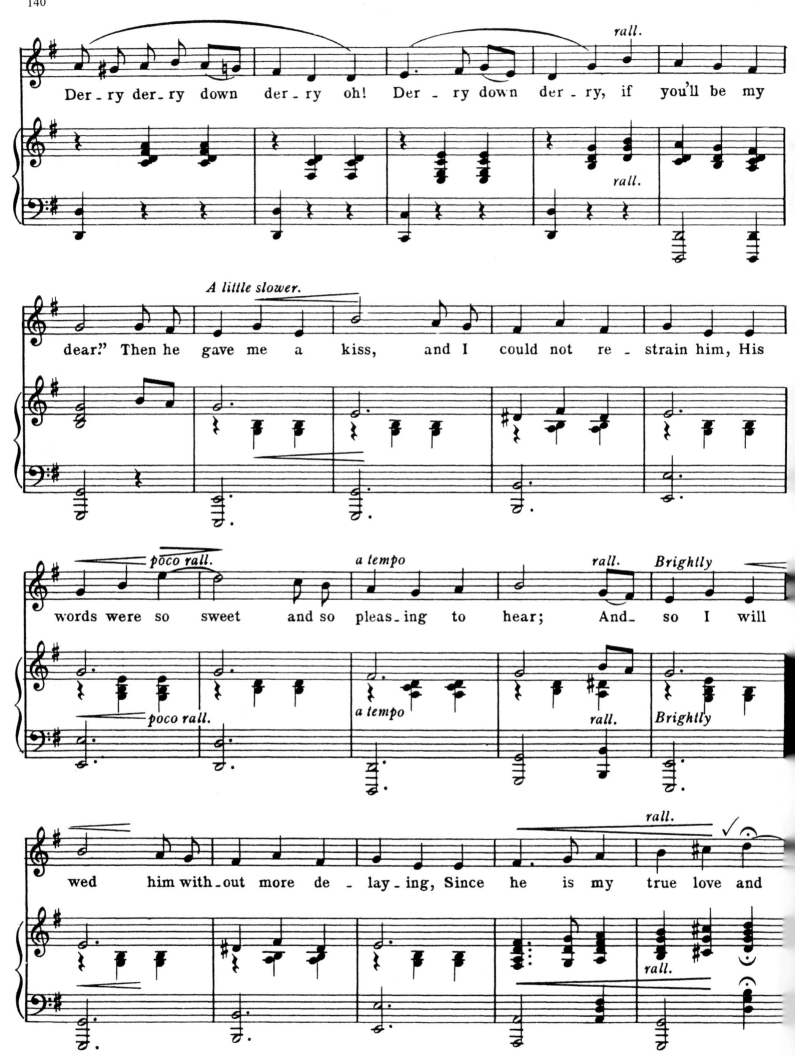

Der - ry der - ry down der - ry oh! Der - ry down der - ry, if you'll be my

rall.

A little slower.

dear." Then he gave me a kiss, and I could not re - strain him, His

poco rall. *a tempo* *rall.* *Brightly*

words were so sweet and so pleas - ing to hear; And so I will

rall.

wed him with - out more de - lay - ing, Since he is my true love and

Tempo I⁰
Very brightly.

AUF DEM MEERE

(On the Ocean)

Heinrich Heine
English by Henry G. Chapman

Robert Franz
Op. 36, No 1.
Original key E major.

Andante sostenuto.

AVE VERUM

(Jesu, Word of God Incarnate)

Wolfgang Amadeus Mozart

BENEATH A WEEPING WILLOW'S SHADE

Francis Hopkinson
arranged by
Harold Milligan

Andante espressivo ♪ = 144

Be - neath a weep - ing wil - low's shade, She
E - cho to___ her strains___ re - plied, The

sat and sang___ a - lone,___ Be - neath___ a weep - ing
winds her sor - rows bore,___ Fond E - cho to___ her

148

THE BLUE-BELL
from "An Old Garden"

Verse by
Margaret Deland

Edward MacDowell

BIST DU BEI MIR

(You Are With Me)

Anonymous
translation by Hansel Powell

J. S. Bach

Bist du bei mir, geh' ich mit Freu - den
You are with me, my joy for - ev - er.

zum Ster - ben und zu mei - ner Ruh', zum Ster - ben und zu mei - ner
Un - til my death and un - to my rest, un - til my death and un - to

Ruh'. Bist du bei mir, geh' ich mit
rest. You are with me, my joy for

Printed in the USA by G. Schirmer, Inc.

Freu - den zum Ster - ben __ und zu mei - ner __ Ruh', zum __
ev - er. Un - til __ my __ death and un - to my rest, un -

Ster - ben und zu mei - ner Ruh'. Ach, wie ver - gnügt
till __ death and un - to rest. Oh how con - tent

wär' so mein En - de, Es drück - ten __ dei - ne schö - nen __
all of my earth - ly days, And at __ the __ end will your __ per - fect

Hän - de mir __ die ge - treu - en Au - gen zu. Ach, wie ver -
lov - ing hand reach to __ gent - ly __ close my eyes. Oh how con -

gnügt wär' so mein En - de, Es drück - ten
tent all of my days And at the

dei - ne schö - nen Hän - de mir die ge-treu - en Au - gen zu.
end will your per - fect lov - ing hand reach to gent - ly close my eyes.

Bist du bei mir, geh' ich mit Freu - den,
You are with me, my joy for - e - ver.

zum Ster - ben und zu mei - ner Ruh', zum Ster - ben und zu mei - ner Ruh'.
Un - til my death and un - to my rest, un - til death and un - to rest.

THE CAROL OF THE BIRDS

text by the composer

John Jacob Niles

Christ - mas day in the morn - ing, cu - roo, cu - roo, cu - roo, _____ cu -

roo, cu - roo, _ cu - roo. _____ The lark, the dove, the red - bird came, cu -

roo, cu - roo, cu - roo, ___ The lark, the dove, the red - bird came And

158

owl was there, his eyes so wide As he did sit at sweet Ma-ry's side On

Christ-mas day in the morn - ing, cu - roo, cu-roo, cu - roo,_____ cu-

roo, cu - roo, cu - roo._____ The shep-herd knelt up - on the hay, cu-

roo, cu - roo, __ cu - roo, __ The shep-herd knelt up - on the hay, As

an - gels sang the night a-way And God pro-claim-ed the ho - ly day, cu-

roo, cu - roo, cu - roo, __ cu - roo, cu - roo, cu - roo. __

CARMEÑA

Ellis Walton

H. Lane Wilson

C'EST MON AMI

(My Friend)

translation by Alice Mattullath

Old French Air
arranged by Bainbridge Crist

know-ing him your love grows fond - er, Bring him to me,
aime en - sui - te da - van - ta - ge: C'est mon a - mi,

riten. *a tempo*

lov - ers are we! I have his heart and mine has he;
ren - dez - le moi! J'ai son a - mour, il a ma foi;

rit. *a tempo*

I have his heart and mine has he._____
J'ai son a - mour, il a ma foi._____

rit. *a tempo*

If he can wake the ech - oes sleep - ing With - in the
Si, par sa voix ten - dre et plain - ti - ve, Il char -

heart and mine has he.
mour, il a ma foi.

If to some poor and need-y
Si pas-sant près de sa chau-miè-

broth-er, Who is not young and strong of limb, And
re Le pauvre, en voy-ant son trou-peau,

CLOUDS

Author unknown

Ernest Charles

One lit-tle hour we know their grace— They pass like shad-ows, nor hold their

place, Ev - er re-cur-ring, like the dawn,

Nev-er en-dur-ing, but al-ways gone, Part of the in-fi-nite, shall we say,

Part of the mo-ment we call to - day.

Clouds a-drift in the sum - mer sky

Re-sem-ble Life, as they wan - der by.

COME YE BLESSED

from *The Holy City*

Matthew 25:34

Alfred Gaul

Then shall the King say, Come, come. Come, ye bless - ed, ye bless - ed of My Fa - ther, in - her - it the king - dom, in - her - it the king - dom pre-par'd for you, for____ you.

CRÉPUSCULE
(Twilight)

Armand Silvestre
English version by
Lorraine Noel Finley

Jules Massenet

DANNY BOY

Fred E. Weatherly

Old Irish Air

Oh, Dan-ny Boy, the pipes,the pipes are call - ing.......... From glen to

glen, and down the moun-tain side,............................. The sum-mer's

DREAM VALLEY

William Blake

Roger Quilter

ELÉGIE

Louis Gallet
translation by Alice Mattullath

Jules Massenet

DAS ERSTE VEILCHEN
(The First Violet)

from *Egon Erbert*
by W. Bartholomew

Felix Mendelssohn

breast.
Brust.

cresc.

dim. ritard.

pp

pp

The Spring is de-part-ed, the vio-let is dead,
Der Lenz ist vor-ü-ber, das Veil-chen ist tot,

a tempo.

pp

the vio-let is dead! Flow-ers more gay now deck its
das Veil-chen ist tot; rings stehn viel Blu-men, blau und

cresc. *sf* *p* *cresc.*

bed. Un-heed-ed they blossom, in mem'ry I see The vio-let, the
rot, ich ste-he in mit-ten, und se-he sie kaum, ich ste-he in-

sf *sf* *cresc.* *sf*

ES MUSS EIN WUNDERBARES SEIN

(It Must Be Wonderful)

Oscar von Redwitz

Franz Liszt

Es muss ein Wun-der-ba-res sein
The love that link-eth soul to

sein um's Lie-ben zwei-er See-len, sich schlie-ssen
soul Must be a won-drous feel-ing; The two but

ganz ein-an-der ein, sich nie ein Wort ver-heh-len;
halves of one sweet whole, Each nought from each con-ceal-ing.

und Freud' und Leid,___ und Glück und Not___
And ev-'ry joy___ or woe of heart___

GOTT IM FRÜHLING

(God in Springtime)

J. P. Uz
translation by Lorraine Noel Finley

Franz Schubert

KEINE SORG' UM DEN WEG

(Love Finds Out the Way)

J. Raff

A LEGEND

Pleshtchéyeff
translated by Nathan Haskell Dole

Pyotr Il'yich Tchaikovsky

Printed in the USA by G. Schirmer, Inc.

He wa-tered them three times a day　To make a
Il les soi-gnait a-vec a-mour,　Vou-lant s'en

gar-land for his hair.　And when in time the
faire u-ne cou-ron-ne.　Mais des en-fants du

ros-es bloomed,　He called the chil-dren in to
voi-si-na-ge　É-tant ve-nus un beau ma-

share:　They tore the flow'rs from ev-'ry stem,
tin,　Ont mis les ro-ses au pil-la-ge

204

And left the gar - den stript and bare. "How wilt thou weave__ thy-
Et dé - vas - té tout le jar - din. «Pau - vre cou - ron - ne, com -

self a crown Now that thy ros - es are all dead?"
ment la fai - re? Les beaux ro - siers n'ont plus de fleurs!»

"Ye have for - got - ten that the thorns_____ Are left for me," the
«Mais les é - pi - nes sont res - té - es,_____ ré - pond Jé - sus, ce -

Christ - child said. They plait - ed then a crown of
la suf - fit.» Puis, en cou - ron - ne les tres -

thorns, And laid it rude - ly on his head.
sant, Sur ses che - veux il la po - sa.

A gar - land for his fore - head made,__ For ros - es
Gout - tes de sang, au lieu de ro - ses, Sou - dain bril -

drops of blood in - stead!
lè - - rent sur son front!

THE LOVELY SONG MY HEART IS SINGING

text by the composer

Edmund Goulding

drift - ing down on beams of moon - light, To

rest with - in our mo - ment, my be - lov - ed, When

I'm a - lone, it's soft and plead - ing, When

you ____ are here my whole world rings!_____ The

ech - o of that mo-ment al - ways brings the

love - ly song that my heart sings.____

MYSTERY'S SONG

from *The Fairy Queen*

E. Settle
after *A Midsummer Night's Dream*
by William Shakespeare

Henry Purcell

Original Key C mi.

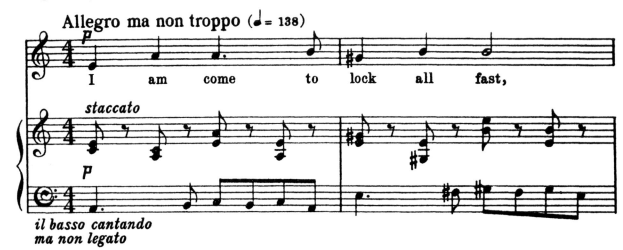

MARIÄ WIEGENLIED
(The Virgin's Slumber Song)

Martin Boelitz
English version by Edward Teschemacher

Max Reger

214

NYMPHS AND SHEPHERDS

Thomas Shadwell

Henry Purcell

Printed in the USA by G. Schirmer, Inc.

f con anima

Nymphs and shep-herds, come_ a - way, come a - way,

Nymphs and shep-herds, come_ a - way, come a - way, come

come, come,_ come_ a - way! In ye grove, in ye grove let's sport and

play, let's sport_ and play, let's sport_ and play! For

danc_ing, to mu - - - sic, to danc_ing, to

leggiero

cresc.

mu - - - - - - sic and to po - et_ry.

dim.

l. h.

p dolce

mf

dim.

Your flock may now, now, now, now, now, now, now, now, now,

dim.

tranquillo

cresc.

molto cresc.

now, se - cure_ly__ rove;___ Whilst you ex - press, whilst

mf leggiero

REND' IL SERENO AL CIGLIO
(Bring to Your Eyes)
from *Sosarme*

English version by Joan Boytim

George Frideric Handel

Rend' il se - re - no al ci - gli - o, ma - dre, non pian - ger più, non pian - ger più, nò. ma - dre, non pian - ger più.

Bring to your eyes re - newed calm - ness, moth - er, now weep no more, now weep no more. No! Moth - er, now weep no more.

Rend' il se - re - no al
Bring to your eyes re - newed

221

SEPARAZIONE

(Parting)

Italian Folksong
arranged by
Giovanni Sgambati

English version by
Henry G. Chapman

SÉRÉNADE

(Sing, Smile, Slumber)

Victor Hugo
English version by Willis Wager

Charles Gounod
edited by Carl Deis

En-tends-tu＿＿ ma pen-sé - e Qui te＿＿ ré-pond tout bas?＿＿＿＿＿
Et sou - dain＿＿ le fa-rou-che Soup-çon＿＿ s'é-va-nou - it.＿＿＿＿＿
Has my heart＿＿ ev-er told you The thrill＿ of all your charms?＿＿＿
Jeal-ous fear＿＿ ev-er af - ter Is gone＿and trust finds room.＿＿＿

Ton doux chant me rap - pel - le Les plus beaux de mes jours.＿＿＿＿
Ah! le ri - re fi - dè - le Prouve un cœur sans dé - tours.＿＿＿＿
Your sweet voice is re - call - ing That long since van-ished day.＿＿＿＿
Your frank smile so dis - arm - ing Shows a heart fair as May.＿＿＿＿

Ah!＿＿＿＿＿＿＿＿＿＿ Chan - tez, chan - tez,＿＿ ma bel - le, Chan -
Ah!＿＿＿＿＿＿＿＿＿＿ Ri - ez, ri - ez,＿＿ ma bel - le, Ri -
Ah,＿＿＿＿＿＿＿＿＿ sing on; sing on,＿＿ en - thrall - ing, Sing
Ah,＿＿＿＿＿＿＿＿＿ smile on, smile on,＿＿ thou charm - ing, Smile

3. Quand tu dors,_____ cal-me et pu-re Dans l'om - bre sous mes yeux,_____
3. *When you dream,_____ sleep-ing sweet-ly While I guard your re - pose,_____*

— Ton ha-lei - ne mur-mu-re Des mots_ har-mo-ni-
— *Then I hear_____ you com-plete-ly Your love_ for me dis-*

eux._____ Ton beau corps se ré-vè-le Sans voi - le et
close._____ Your fair beau-ty in splen-dor Then shines with

sans a - tours._____ Ah!_____ Dor-
pur - est ray._____ Ah,_____ dream

230

THE SLEEP THAT FLITS ON BABY'S EYES

Rabindranath Tagore

John Alden Carpenter

SPRING IS AT THE DOOR

Nora Hopper

Roger Quilter

Spring is at the door: She bears a gold-en store, Her maund with yel-low daf-fo-dils run-neth o'er Her

236

DIE STILLE
(Silence)

Joseph, Freiherr von Eichendorff
translation by Theodore Baker

Robert Schumann

Moderato, sempre pianissimo.

Es weiss und räth es doch Kei-ner, wie mir so wohl ist, so wohl! Ach
There's none can know it or feel it, How all my heart is a-glow! Ah,

wüsst' es nur Ei-ner, nur Ei-ner, kein Mensch es sonst wis-sen sollt'. So
on-ly to one would I tell it, And no-bod-y else should know. So

still ist's nicht draussen im Schnee, so stumm und ver-schwiegen sind die
si-lent the snow does not lie, So mute and so qui-et are Not

Ster-ne nicht in der Höh', als mei-ne Ge-dan-ken sind.___ Ich
e'en the stars in the sky As the thoughts that I'm thinking are.___ I

DIE STILLE WASSERROSE
(The Silent Waterlily)

E. Giebel
Translation by Theodore Baker

Alexander von Fielitz

WEEP NO MORE

from *Hercules*

John Fletcher

George Frideric Handel

244

wing - ed dreams fly fast, Why should sad-ness long - er

last? Weep no more, weep no more, Joys as wing - ed

dim. cresc. *p*

pp

dreams fly fast, Why should sad - ness long - er last?

p

Why, why, why, why should sad - ness long - er last?

TE DEUM
(Vouchsafe, O Lord)

English version by
R. L. Beckhard

George Frideric Handel

nos - tri Do-mi-ne, mi - se-re - re. Fi - at mi-se - ri-
Lord,__ be mer-ci-ful, Lord, have mer-cy. Lord, let Thy mer - cy

cor - dia tu - a su-per nos quem-ad - mo - dum spe-ra - vi-mus,
be __ up-on us, be up-on us, O Lord, as we trust in Thee,

quem-ad-mo-dum spe - ra - vi-mus in te.
as our trust is in_ Thee, our trust in Thee.

WHEN I HAVE OFTEN HEARD
YOUNG MAIDS COMPLAINING
from *The Fairy Queen*

E. Settle
after *A Midsummer Night's Dream*
by William Shakespeare

Henry Purcell

THE WILLOW SONG

from *Othello*
by William Shakespeare

Arthur Sullivan

WIND OF THE WHEAT

Harold Simpson

Montague F. Phillips

dawn, It whis-pers in the dawn.

It sings a low sweet song The whole day

long: As love once sang to me Of

joys that used to be. The

THE
FIRST
BOOK OF
MEZZO-SOPRANO/ALTO
SOLOS
PART III

PREFACE

The First Book of Solos series has been compiled to meet requests of voice teachers who have expressed a need for more beginning vocal literature similar to the "Part I" and "Part II" books. This repertoire speaks to students who may have successfully sung songs from the *Easy Songs for Beginning Singers* series. Those students who have used *The First Book of Solos – Part I and Part II*, may still find that this level of song material is appropriate before venturing into the volumes of *The Second Book of Solos*. This new "Part III" may also suffice as a beginning book for certain students, or serve as a companion to "Part I" and "Part II." Since the level is the same for *The First Book of Solos – Part I, Part II and Part III*, a student can begin in any of the books.

The first two volumes were released in 1991 and 1993. Since then, some excellent songs have passed into the "Public Domain" category. It is significant that songs such as "The Green Cathedral," "Waters Ripple and Flow," "A Brown Bird Singing," "When I Think Upon the Maidens," "The Ships of Arcady," "May-Day Carol," and "The Time for Making Songs Has Come" have become available for young singers.

The anthologies in "Part III" contain 34 to 36 songs appropriate to specific voice types, and in suitable keys. The basic format provides songs of many styles from the baroque era into the 20th century. In addition to many familiar standard art songs, there are a number of unfamiliar gems, such as "The Bubble Song," the trilogy "At the Zoo," "Bluebird," "The Little Old Lady in Lavender Silk," "Maidens Are Like the Wind," "Sing a Song of Sixpence," and "When Big Profundo Sang Low C." In keeping with the original format, there are many American and British songs, as well as a good sampling of Italian, German and French art songs (with singable translations). Some favorites include "Invictus," "Come Back to Sorrento," "Vilia," and "I Walked Today Where Jesus Walked." As in the other books of the series, a few sacred solos are included. Many songs in "Part III" were previously obtainable in only sheet form or have been long out of print. In order to include songs represented by the 1916 to 1922 year span, several of the accompaniments and songs may prove to be a bit more of a challenge than in "Part I" and "Part II."

The First Book of Solos – Part III concludes this series of five books for each voice type, with no song duplication (*The First Book of Solos – Part I, Part II, Part III, The Second Book of Solos – Part I, Part II*). The number of songs in the twenty volumes totals 668. The average number of songs presented for each voice numbers approximately 167. This presents a wide smorgasbord of vocal literature for studio and performance use for student singers at most any age.

G. Schirmer is to be commended for allowing this series of vocal solos to grow substantially. Wherever I meet teachers who have used these many books, they express profound thanks for them, and acknowledge that their availability makes repertoire demands so much easier to manage. May you and your students enjoy the new choices made available in this anthology.

Joan Frey Boytim
June, 2005

CONTENTS

259

for Miss Kitty Cheatham
AT THE ZOO

Burges Johnson

Arthur Walter Kramer
(1890-1969)

I. The Porcupine

It must be hard for ___ you, por-cu-pine, To dress when the day be - gins, I'm glad there_ are-n't an-y clothes of mine A - need-in' so man - y pins.

II. The Snake

Lightly

A snake's the fun - ni - est

thing I know, So dread - ful - ly in - com -

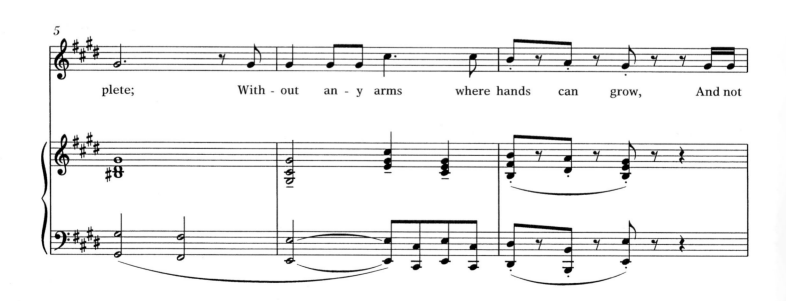

plete; With - out an - y arms where hands can grow, And not

III. The Giraffe

But when the jam and the cook - ie jar Are hid on the high - est shelf, _____ I wish't I was as tall as you crea - tures are, In - stead of my ti - ny self. _____

BEAU SOIR
(Afterglow)

Paul Bourget
English version by Deems Taylor

Claude Debussy
(1862-1918)

Andante ma non troppo

Lorsque au so - leil cou - chant les ri -
When in the set - ting sun glow the

viè - res sont ro - ses, Et qu'un tiè - de fris -
riv - u - lets gold - en, When a thrill soft - ly

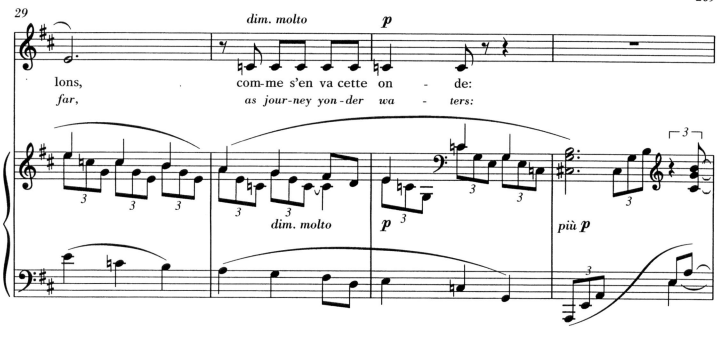

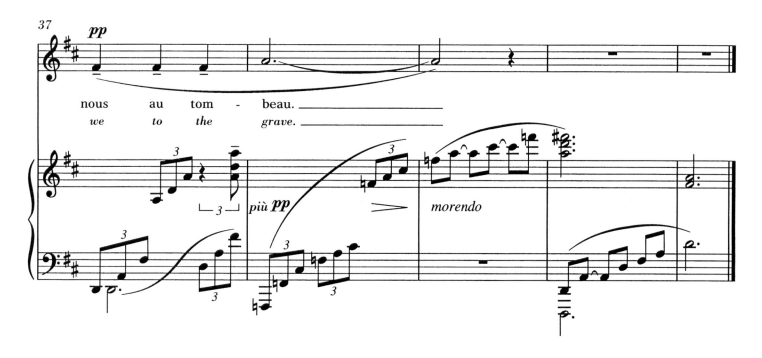

to Alice B. Cobbold
THE BUBBLE SONG

Mabel Dearmer

Martin Shaw
(1875-1958)

height. Here for a mo - ment, then a -

way, _____ The rose - col - oured bub - ble has had ___ his

day.

Bub - bles of

17
glo - ry, bub-bles of gain, Float-ing a - way from a cas - tle in Spain,

19
Bub-bles that fall from the clouds _ a - bove, Del - i - cate pris - ms, bub-bles of

21 *a little slower*
love, Here for a mo - ment, then __ a -

23
way, _____ The bub - ble is bro - ken, ah, well - a -

BUT THE LORD IS MINDFUL OF HIS OWN

from *St. Paul*

Felix Mendelssohn
(1809-1847)

BY DIMPLED BROOK

John Milton

Thomas Augustine Arne
(1710-1778)

sweet, the cheer - ing __ cup and con - verse sweet. Night has __ o - ther joys in

store, skies with __ jew - els stud - ded o'er.

Tune - ful voic - es, twink - ling feet, The cheer - ing __ cup, and __ con - verse

sweet the cheer - ing __ cup, and con - verse sweet.

CLAIR DE LUNE
(Moonlight)

Paul Verlaine
English version by Marion Farquhar

Gabriel Fauré
(1845-1924)

Votre âme est un pa-y-sa-ge choi-si
Your soul is a gar-den, rare and most choice

Que vont char-mant mas - ques et ber-ga-mas - ques _____
With stat-u-esque mask - ers, grace-ful-ly plas - tic, _____

sempre cantabile

Jou - ant du luth et dan - sant et qua-si
Play - ing the lute as they dance, and sem - i -

Ped. * Ped. * Ped. * Ped. * Ped. * Ped. *

284

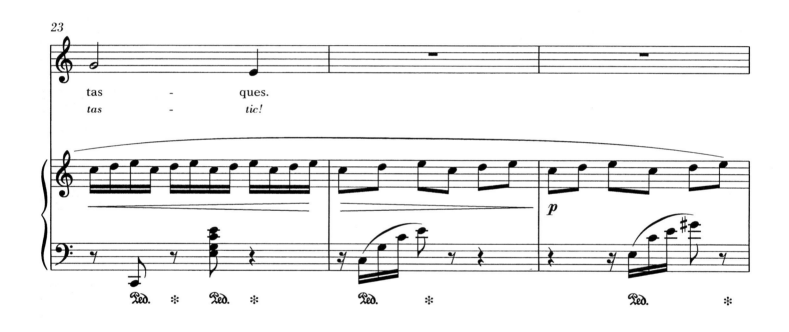

29

— et la — vie op - por - tu - - - ne,
— and life — most op - por - tune, _____

31

Ils n'ont pas l'air de croire à leur bon -
They yet ap - pear to feel their joy is

34

heur Et leur chan - son se mêle au clair de
vain, And their re - frain is blend - ed with the

36

lu - ne.
moon! _____

decresc.

pp

Ped.

CORALS

Zoë Akins

Bryceson Treharne
(1879-1948)

In a gently flowing style

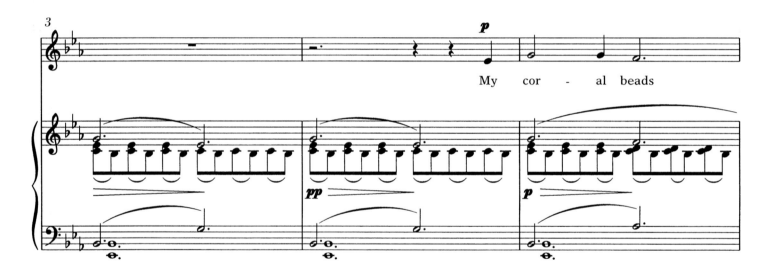

My cor - al beads

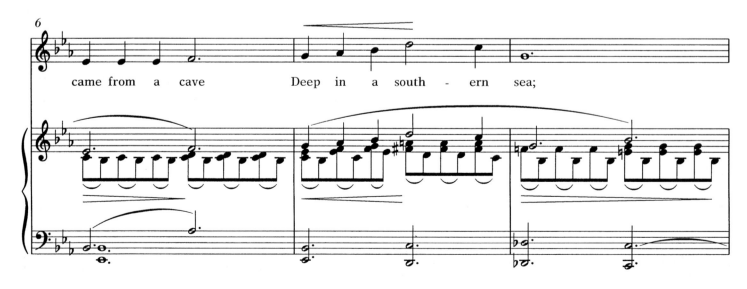

came from a cave Deep in a south - ern sea;

DOLCE SCHERZA
(Sweetly play)

Giacomo Antonio Perti
(1661-1756)

Andantino

Dol - ce scher - za e dol - ce ri - de

Va - go lab - bro e spi - ra a - mor; Ma t'al -

let - ta e poi t'uc - ci - de Co - si af -

Dolce scherza e dolce ride
Vago labbro e spira amor;
Ma t'alletta e poi t'uccide

Sweetly play and sweetly smiles
the charming lip breathes love;
but it entices you and then kills you

Cosi affligge questo cor.

Thus it afflicts this heart.

EVENING SONG

Clara Edwards
(1887-1974)

IF THERE WERE DREAMS TO SELL

Thomas Lovell Beddoes

John Ireland
(1879-1962)

Moderato

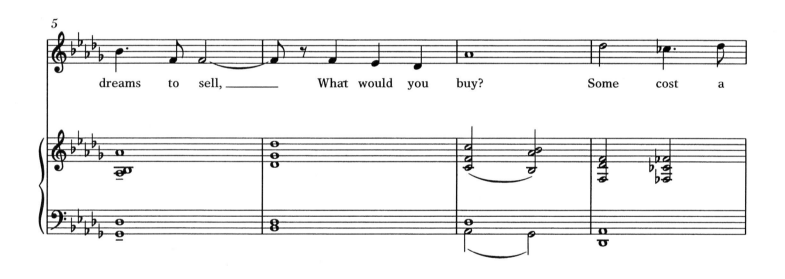

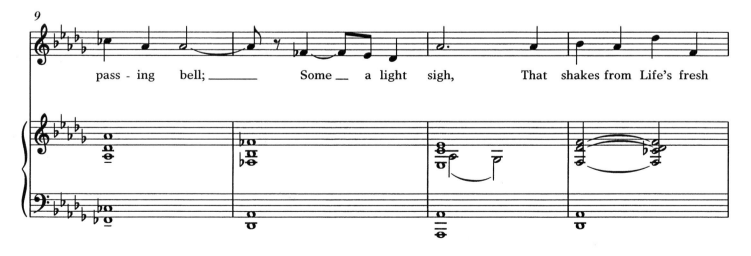

to A.A.T.

I WALKED TODAY WHERE JESUS WALKED

Daniel S. Twohig*

Geoffrey O'Hara
(1882-1967)

*Words used by exclusive permission

lit - tle lanes, they have not changed— A sweet peace fills the

air. I walked to-day where Je- sus walked, ____ And

felt His pres - ence there. My

ICH LIEBE DICH
(I Love Thee)

Hans Christian Andersen
German version by F. von Holstein
English version by Auber Forestier

Edvard Grieg
(1843-1907)

Er - den,/heav - en,/len - ken,/turn - ing, } ich lie - be dich, ich lie - be dich, ich lie - be dich in Zeit und
I love but thee, I love but thee, I love but thee through all e -

E - wig-keit! Ich lie - be dich in Zeit und E - wig-keit!
ter - ni - ty! I love but thee through all e - ter - ni - ty!

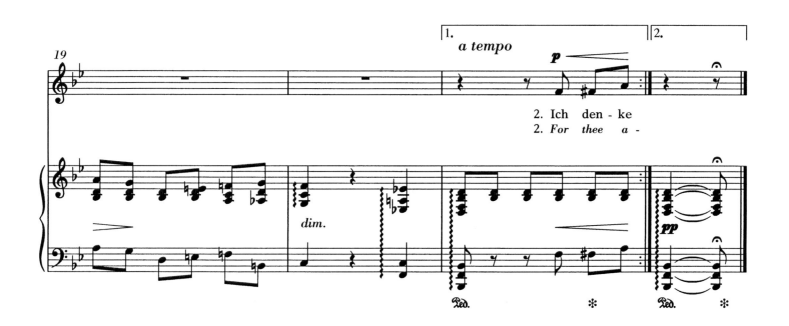

2. Ich den - ke
2. For thee a -

LANDSCAPE

Poem by Sada-ihe
Japanese (13th century)

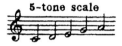

Charles T. Griffes
(1884-1920)

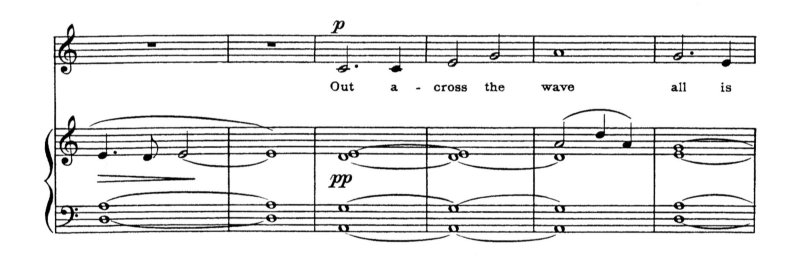

THE LARK NOW LEAVES HIS WATERY NEST

William Davenant

Horatio Parker
(1863-1919)

beau - ty __ at your __ eyes.

The mer - chant bows un -

to the sea - man's star _____

The plough-man from the sun his sea - son takes.

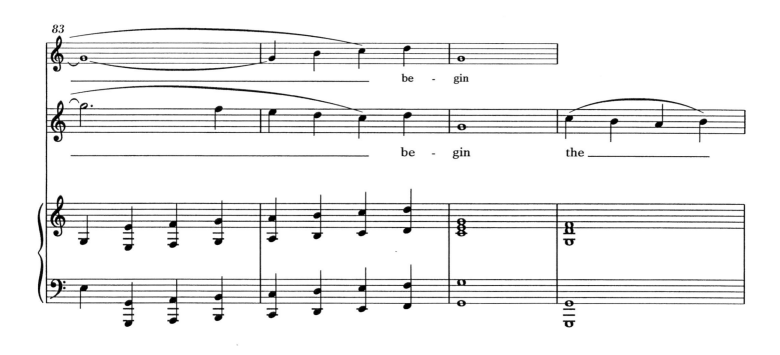

THE LITTLE OLD LADY IN LAVENDER SILK

Dorothy Parker*

Mary Margaret Vinmont

*From "Not So Deep as a Well" by Dorothy Parker (copyright, 1926, 1928, 1931, and 1936; published by The Viking Press, Inc.

bol - i - cal) flood and si - moom._____ When you come to this time of a - bate - ment, To this pass - ing from sum - mer to fall,_____ It is man - ners to is - sue a state - ment As to what you got out of it all._____ So I'll

318

320

THE LOTUS BLOOM

Anonymous adaptation from the Chinese

John Jacob Niles
(1892-1980)

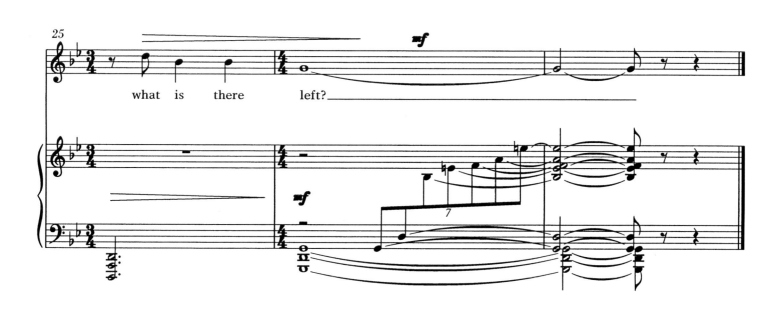

LORD, HOW LONG WILT THOU FORGET ME?

Adapted from Psalm 13

Ranzzini
(1747-1810)

Lord, how long wilt Thou forget me? Lord, how

MENUET D'EXAUDET
(Exaudet's Minuet)

French words by Favart
English version by Sigmund Spaeth

André-Joseph Exaudet
(1710-1752)

MIT EINER WASSERLILIE
(With a Water Lily)

Henrik Ibsen

Edvard Grieg
(1843-1907)

60

mf *poco ten.*

Li - lien spie - len ob der Tie - fe,
Lil - ies play a - bove the deep,

mf

poco ten.

63

poco ten.

Neck ist still, als ob er schlie - fe.
Wat - er - sprites but feign to sleep.

poco ten.

66 *poco rit.*   *p a tempo*

Sieh, Ma - ri - a, was ich
See, Ma - ri - a, what I'm

p

69

brin - ge: Blu - me
bring - ing Lil - ies

MORGEN!
(Tomorrow)

John Henry Mackay
English version by Florence Easton

Richard Strauss
(1864-1949)

Langsam

sehr getragen

sehr ruhig

Und mor - gen wird die Son - ne wie - der
To - mor - row morn a - gain we'll see the

MORGEN-HYMNE

(Morning Hymn)

Robert Reinick
English version by Theodore Baker

George Henschel
(1850-1934)

MY LOVER IS A FISHERMAN

Lily Strickland
(1887-1958)

346

STILL WIE DIE NACHT
(Still as the night)

English version by M.J. Barnett

Karl Böhm
(1844-1920)

17

soll dei - ne Lie - be, dei - ne Lie - be sein,
Thy love would be, Thy love would be for me,

21 *pp* *poco rit.* *a tempo*

soll dei - ne Lie - be sein!
Thy love would be for me.

pp

25 *poco rit.* *a tempo* *mf*

Wenn du mich liebst,
Lov - est thou me,

mf

30 *p* *rit.*

so wie ich dich, will ich dein ei - gen
Then love I thee, And all thine own I'll

DER NUßBAUM
(The Walnut Tree)

Julius Mosen
English version by Florence Easton

Robert Schumann
(1810-1856)

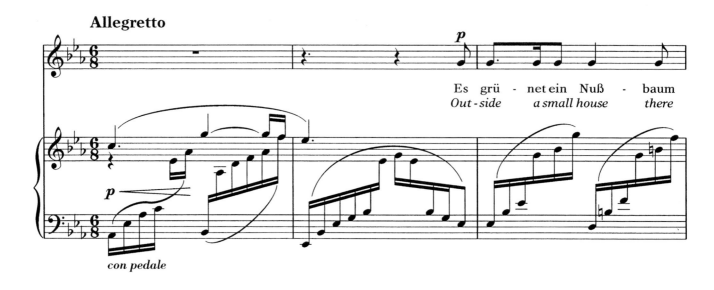

* This is the word in Mosen's poem. Schumann substituted the word "Blätter."

22

p

Es flü - stern je zwei zu zwei ge - paart,
They whis - per in pairs,   each   pair   a - part,

25

nei - gend, beu - gend
Bend - ing gen - tly em -

28

zier - lich   zum Kus - se die Häupt - chen zart.
brac - ing,   and mur - mur-ing, heart   to   heart.

31

rit.   (*a tempo*)   *p*

Sie flü - stern von ei - nem
They whis - per of one   young

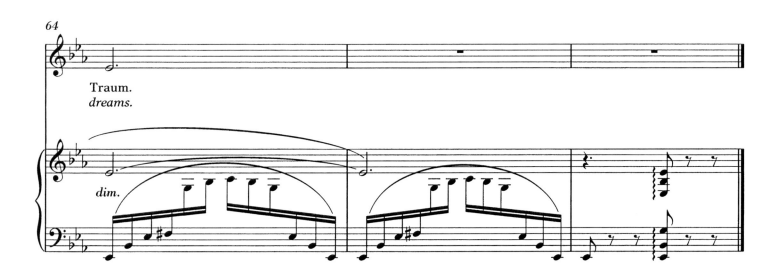

O LOVELY PEACE

from *Judas Maccabaeus*

George Frideric Handel
(1685-1759)

thy___ bless-ings, thy___ bless-ings all___ a-round.

p dolce

Let fleec-y flocks the hills a - dorn,_____ And

val-leys smile with wav - y corn, Let fleec-y flocks the

hills_ a-dorn, And val-leys smile___

with wav-y corn, And smile _____ with

wav - y corn, with wav - y corn,

with wav - y, with wav - y corn, with wav-y

corn. Let fleec-y flocks the

più lento
p

hills a - dorn,⏤ the hills⏤ a - dorn, And

più lento

p

smile⏤

Adagio
mf

smile,⏤ smile,⏤ smile⏤ and⏤ smile,⏤ with wav - y

mf

mf

Tempo I

corn.

p

f

rit.

O PRAISE THE LORD

(Praise the Lord, O my soul)

Maurice Greene
(1696-1755)

Vivace

O praise the Lord, _ ye an - gels _ of his, _ ye an - gels _ of his, _ ye

to Louis and Dinah de Glehn

OVER THE LAND IS APRIL

Robert Louis Stevenson

Roger Quilter
(1877-1953)

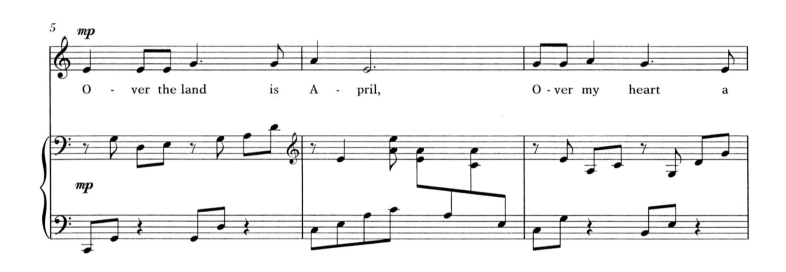

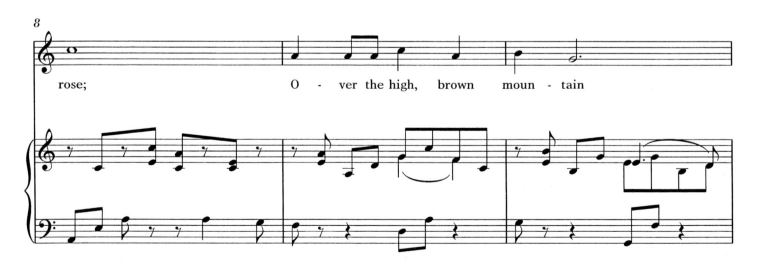

25
high - way, love, and by - way The snows suc - ceed the

p dolce

28
rose. O - ver the high, brown moun - tain

poco cresc.

poco cresc.

31
The wind of win - ter blows.

34
p
Say, love, do you hear me, Hear my son - nets

p

ring?

O - ver the high, brown moun - tain

cresc.

cresc.

I sound the song of spring.

f

pochiss. rit.

dim.

p a tempo

O - ver the land is A - pril, O - ver my heart a rose;

p

to Viola Karlson Byrgerson

PRAYER OF THE NORWEGIAN CHILD

Olaf Trojörgson

Richard Kountz
(1896-1950)

Poco più mosso

Lord Je - sus, think on__ me; Make my__ soul like un-to Thee.

p a tempo

Lord__ Je - sus, think on__ me; Make my__ soul

1. rit.

like__ un-to Thee.

2. rit.

like__ un-to Thee.__

PREMIÈRE DANSE
(The First Dance)

Jacques Normand
English version by Henry G. Chapman

Jules Massenet
(1842-1912)

Brioso, allegro, leggero

Des bons vieux airs très con - nus
To   a   good   old   well - known air,

Mar - quant la ca - den - ce, A - vec des ges - tes me - nus La fil - let - te
Full of pret - ty glanc - es And well in time, this fair Lit - tle maid - en

dan - se.
danc - es.

El - le va, vient, en sau-tant   Tou - jours a - vec grâ - ce,
Light - ly springs the lit - tle dame,   Than a bird a - lert - er;

Et ce jeu nou - veau pour - tant Point ne l'em - bar - ras -
Nev - er - the - less, this new game Does not dis - con - cert

se.
her.

Son pied sur le clair par-quet Glisse ou se dé-
On the shin-ing floor her feet Twin-kle thro' their

robe, Et son pe - tit doigt co - quet ____ Re - lè - ve sa

pac - es, With co - quet - tish fin - gers fleet ____ She rais - es her

ro - be. Cinq

dress - es. Just

ans! et pas de le - çons! Mais c'est ru - sé, da - me!

five! And les - sons had none! But all the wiles, hey _ day!

Et ça vous a des fa - çons De bel - le ma - da - me.

And all the airs, ev - 'ry one, Of an - y fine la - dy.

Ça se **cambre** a - vec or - gueil, Ça vous prend des po - ses,
How she preens with pride, this mite! How her pose com - pels you!

Et dé - jà, du coin de l'œil, Ça vous dit des cho - ses.
And with the tail of her eye Man - y things she tells you.

Ça vous dit: «Re - gar - dez - moi Tour - ner et sou - ri - re;
Ah! says she, Just look at me! Who would not de - sire me?

poco ritard. **p**

Je suis char - mante et, ma foi! J'ai - me qu'on m'ad - mi - re!
I'm ve - ry charm - ing and want you all to ad - mire me!

poco ritard. **p**

SAPPHISCHE ODE
(Sapphic Ode)

Hans Schmidt
English version by Arthur Westbrook

Johannes Brahms
(1833-1897)

Ziemlich langsam

SINCE FIRST I MET THEE

Anton Rubinstein
(1829-1894)

Long years have winged their wear-y flight Since first I met thee, And though en-shrined with-in my

heart, I'd fain for-get thee; For as the clouds a-round the sun ob-scure its bright - ness,

So thou hast robbed my once glad life of all its light - ness!

Oh, world so won - drous fair, Oh, heart, once free from care!

From out my in - most soul es - capes a sigh: ___ From me now all hath flown,

That could in life a - tone For wea - ry hours of an - guish long gone by.

SLUMBER SONG
(Berceuse)

English version by Charles Fonteyn Manney
French version by J. Sergennois

Alexander Gretchaninoff
(1864-1956)

SPIAGGE AMATE

(Beloved Shore)

from *Paride ed Elena*

Raniero de Calzabigi
English version by Joan Boytim

Christoph Willibald von Gluck
(1714-1787)

TO COME, O LORD, TO THEE

W.C. Dix

William Stickles

UN COR DA VOI FERITO

(A heart that thou hast wounded)

from *La Rosaura*

Giovanni Battista Lucini

Alessandro Scarlatti
(1660-1725)